Samsung Galaxy A16

Made Easy Manual

For Beginners

Seniors

Your Complete Step by Step Handbook
for Effortless Mastery — From Setup to
Advanced Tips & Tricks — Everything
You Need to be A Pro.

Pamphy Whyte

Table of Contents

Introduction

Unlock the Future in Your Hands: The Samsung Galaxy A16 User Manual

Welcome to the ultimate guide for mastering the Samsung Galaxy A16—the device that redefines innovation. Packed with cutting-edge features, stunning design, and seamless performance, the Samsung Galaxy A16 is more than a smartphone; it's your gateway to the future. Whether you're a tech enthusiast or a first-time user, this manual is your key to unlocking its full potential. Dive in, explore, and transform the way you connect, create, and conquer every day. The future is at your fingertips—let's get started!

Welcome

The Samsung Galaxy A16 is an excellent smartphone; congrats! Whether you're new to smartphones or want to upgrade, you're about to embark on an exhilarating adventure. Keeping in touch, getting work done, and enjoying entertainment are all made easier than ever before with the Galaxy A16 and its sleek, user-friendly UI.

Here, you will find the key to releasing your device's latent capabilities. As soon as you turn on your phone, you'll find out how to use its easy interface, personalize it to your liking, and delve into its deep capabilities. So that everyone may benefit from the A16's robust features and accessible settings, we have also provided advice for novices and those in their latter years of life.

Is your new phone ready for action? This manual will show you all you need to know to take beautiful pictures, use your smartphone to stay in touch with friends and family on social media, and make it your own.

How about we jump right in and find out how the Samsung Galaxy A16 may improve your daily life?

First Things First

Here you will find the necessary initial steps to set up and use your Samsung Galaxy A16. To guarantee that you are prepared to utilize your phone, let's examine each subject in detail.

Chapter 1: Powering Up Your Samsung A16

Make sure your Samsung Galaxy A16 is fully charged before you dive in, so you can enjoy uninterrupted exploration. The correct way to charge your phone is as follows:

1.Find the Charging Port: When you look down on your Galaxy A16, you should be able to see the charging port. The USB-C charging cable is meant to be inserted here.

2.To Begin Charging, Place the Galaxy A16's charging port on one end of the USB-C cable and the charging adapter on the other. Then, Connect the Adapter to an Electrical Outlet.

3.After you've connected the device, a charging icon will appear on the screen to let you know that it's charging. A percentage of charge will be displayed via the battery icon.

4.Be careful not to overheat the Galaxy A16, as it enables fast charging, which means it will charge faster than ordinary chargers. Upon reaching 100% charge, you are free to remove the plug.

5.Wireless Charging: Unless you know for sure that your Galaxy A16 model supports wireless charging, it's safer to utilize the cable charging option.

6.Charging Time: Depending on the adapter and the use while charging, it usually takes around 1 to 2 hours to charge completely.

The On/Off Switch
To activate your phone, wait until it is fully charged. The following are the power on/off instructions for your Samsung Galaxy A16:

1. Turning On:

o The power button is usually on the side of your device (or the right side in some regions) or on the bottom.

o Keep the Power button pressed for a few seconds or until the Samsung logo shows up on the screen.

Once you see the logo, let go of the button. After the phone powers on, you'll see the Home Screen.

2. Turn Off Power:

o Holding down the Power button for about three seconds will power off the Galaxy A16.

Power Off, Restart, and Emergency Mode are the options that will appear on the screen in a pop-up menu.

Choose OK after tapping Power Off to confirm. At that point, your phone will turn off entirely.

3.**To start over**:

Restarting your device is an option if you have problems or notice that it is operating slowly. All you have to do is choose Restart after pressing and holding the Power button. Rebooting your device in this way will prevent data loss.

Installing the MicroSD and SIM Card

You may extend your storage capacity and connect to mobile networks using a SIM card and a microSD card in your Galaxy A16. The process is as follows:

1.Find the slot for the SIM and microSD card:

A little tray may be found on the left side of the Galaxy A16. The microSD card and SIM card slot is located on this tray.

2.Remove the tray:

A SIM ejector tool or a paperclip will be required to access the tray.

To remove the tray, place the tool into the little hole adjacent to it and give it a little push.

3.Sim Card Insertion:

put the SIM card in the corresponding slot. It ought should snap into position with the gold connections facing downwards. To prevent harm, ensure that the card is facing the right way.

4.A MicroSD Card Insertion Procedure:

Simply place the MicroSD card into the second slot on the tray to increase the storage capacity of your phone. The gold connections, like the SIM card, should be facing downward.

5.Reassembling the tray:

After you've made sure both cards are in, gently put the tray back into the phone. Always make sure it's flush with the device before pushing it in.

6.Getting Everything Ready:

o The SIM and MicroSD cards should be detected automatically by the device once you turn on your phone. Verify that your SIM is active under Settings > Mobile

Networks, then locate the MicroSD card in the Storage section of the Settings menu.

Getting Around the Main Screen
The majority of your interactions with the Samsung Galaxy A16 will take place on the Home Screen. It may be tailored to your needs, and getting to know its layout will make navigating it a breeze:

1.**Introductory Screen:**

o Upon powering up your smartphone, the initial screen that appears is the Home Screen. App icons, widgets (little applications like calendars, weather, etc.), and the status bar make up the interface.

2.Motions using a Swipe or Tap:

o Simply tapping and swiping left or right on the screen will take you to other pages of your Home Screen.

o Launch the associated app or function by tapping on any widget or icon.

3.Navigating to the App Folder:

All of your installed apps may be found in the App Drawer. Swipe up from the screen's bottom to open it.

o The App Drawer also has a Search Bar that you may use to locate files or programs fast.

4.Integrating Add-Ons and Quick Links:

Press and hold an empty area on the screen, then choose Widgets, to add widgets to your Home Screen. After that, pick out a widget that you'd want to have on your home screen.

By grabbing an app's icon and dragging it to a blank spot on the Home Screen, you may also make shortcuts for that app.

5.Making Changes to the Main Screen:

Change the wallpaper, rearrange the apps, or add themes to your Home Screen by going to Settings > Wallpaper and Themes.

Making Sense of the Icons
Numerous icons representing different system operations will be shown on your phone's Home Screen and Status Bar. The following is a list of some of the most important icons:

1.Common Icons for the Status Bar:

Here you may see a series of bars that represent the strength of your mobile network signal at the moment.

o Wi-Fi: If your Wi-Fi is active, it tells you how strong it is. If it's not, it shows you a symbol to let you know.

Battery: shows how much juice is left in the battery. A bolt of lightning represents a charging charge.

To switch on Bluetooth, look for a little "B" symbol. A linked icon will appear when it is paired with a device.

o When you enable the "Do Not Disturb" option, you'll see a symbol that looks like a circle with a line across it.

The usage of location services is indicated by a little map pin icon.

o It is configured to alert when an alarm is activated, as shown by a clock sign.

Notifications: At the top, you'll see icons for several types of notifications, including as incoming messages, app alerts, calendar events, and more.

2.**App Graphics**:

You'll see an icon that graphically represents the purpose of each app on your Home Screen. Take this case in point:

A phone app is represented by a green icon with a white phone sign.

Messages: A text message is symbolized by a blue speech bubble.

The camera app is represented by a camera lens symbol.

3.My **Favorite App Shortcuts**:

You can also personalize the icons for the programs you use most by altering their look or making shortcuts to them.

You can make better use of your phone and quickly access the features you need by getting to know its icons and the layout of the Home Screen.

If you're new to the Samsung Galaxy A16, this section will walk you through the fundamentals so you can start using it straight away.

Methods for Unlocking Your Phone
The initial step in accessing your Samsung Galaxy A16 after powering it on is to unlock

it. The security settings you select determine the ways for unlocking your smartphone. Unlock your phone by following these steps:

1.**On-Screen Power Control**:

Pressing the Power button located on the right side of your phone will wake it up.

Unlocking the phone will be requested after the screen turns on.

2.**Approaches to Unlocking**:

o PIN/Password: Punch in your PIN or password in the text area if you've configured one. You may lock and unlock your phone securely using this way.

If you've configured a pattern lock, all you have to do is trace the pattern you made with your finger.

To unlock your phone using your fingerprint, just place your registered finger on the sensor, which is often on the side or back of the device.

o Facial Recognition: With this feature turned on, all you have to do is glance at your phone to unlock it.

3.Unlock in an Emergency:

If you've linked your Google account and forget your PIN, password, or pattern, you may reset the lock by following the on-screen instructions or utilizing the recovery options on your phone.

First-Time Device Configuration
Start by finishing the initial setup on your Samsung Galaxy A16 when you turn it on for the first time. The first step is this:

1.Geographical Area and Language:

o To change the language, the phone will prompt you. Pick your preferred language by tapping on it from the list. You have the option to select a different language from the dropdown menu; English is often the default.

o You'll be asked to pick your Region (country) when you choose your language. Language, currency, and time zone choices are all determined by this.

2.Configuring Wi-Fi:

o Linking your mobile device to a wireless network follows the process of choosing your area. The phone can find nearby Wi-Fi hotspots. Make sure you choose your home Wi-Fi network.

If prompted, input your Wi-Fi password, and then hit the Connect button. Connecting can be a little slow at first.

3.Update for Software:

After you link your Galaxy A16 to the internet, it could look for upgrades to its software. You should always apply the most recent available updates for your phone's operating system to keep it working smoothly.

4.Services provided by Google:

o After that, log in using your Google account. Log in with your email and password if you already have a Google account. A new Google account can be created during setup if you do not already have one.

Some Google services, such location tracking, backup, and sync, may ask you to activate or disable them.

5.Samsung Store:

o A Samsung Account login is required, albeit it is currently optional. Samsung Pay, Find My Mobile, and Samsung Cloud are all made easier with this account.

6.End of Setup:

If you choose to recover data (such as contacts, images, and applications) from an earlier device, you will be invited to do so after these steps. If you have a backup of your Google Account, you may use it to restore, or you can start again without transferring any data.

After you finish configuring your phone, it will take you to the Home Screen, where you can begin using it!

Picking the Right Language and Area

One of the initial stages in setting up your phone is selecting your language and area. To make the appropriate decisions, follow these steps:

1.**Importance of the Matter**:

Language: By selecting the appropriate language, you can make sure that all the menus, messages, and settings are shown in the language that you like. You have the option to change the language in the settings later on if you want.

o Location: The time zone, currency format, and location-specific applications or services on the phone can be changed using the region setting. To provide just a few examples, your area dictates the version of the app store that you can access, and it can also influence the news and search results that you see.

2.Procedures for Language and Region Selection:

· A list of supported languages will appear when you initially set up your phone. To choose a different language, just scroll down the list and touch on it (for example, English, Spanish, or French).

After you've chosen your language, hit the Next button. On the following screen, you will see a set of nations or areas. Pick the area that matches where you are. If you're currently in the US, for instance, choose US.

You may use this to adjust several parameters, such as the time zone and date format.

3.Future Methods for Altering the Language or Region:

You may access the Settings menu, then go to General Management, and finally, Language and Input if you wish to modify the language or region.

Choose a language to use on your phone's screen or add a new one here. Simply navigate to Settings > General Management > area, then choose the desired nation or area to modify the default setting.

Joining a wireless network

You may get better internet speeds and save mobile data by connecting your Samsung

Galaxy A16 to Wi-Fi. The process is as follows:

1.Make Wi-Fi Active:

o To access the Quick Settings panel, swipe down from the top of the screen.

Please locate the Wi-Fi symbol. Pressing it will activate Wi-Fi if it isn't already on. Another option is to activate Wi-Fi by going to Settings > Connections > Wi-Fi.

2.Network Selection:

o After a short while, your phone will have compiled a list of all the Wi-Fi networks in the area.

Choose your Wi-Fi network (for example, your home Wi-Fi) and tap on it. The presence of a password prompt indicates that the network in question is private.

3.Login with your password:

· Be cautious while entering your Wi-Fi password (it is case-sensitive).

> Press the Connect button. The Wi-Fi symbol in the status bar will become solid if the password is valid, and your phone will connect to the Wi-Fi network.

4.Issue Resolution:

Verify the correct operation of the Wi-Fi router and the accuracy of the password entered if the phone still fails to connect.

You might also attempt turning off the network and then rejoining again, or you could try rebooting your router.

5. **check the Link**:

o Launch a web browser or an internet-dependent program like Google or YouTube to check the connection. Your wireless network is operational if the app can successfully load the content.

Your Google Account Login

To use Gmail, the Google Play Store, and Google Drive, among other Google services, you must log into your Google Account on your Samsung Galaxy A16. Authentication is as follows:

1.**While setting up, sign in**:

When you first set everything up, Google will ask you to log in using your Google Account. Just type in your email and password to access your Google account (like Gmail).

2.**Create an account with Google**:

o To create a Google account, just click the "Create Account" button when prompted during login. Enter your name, select an email provider (Gmail is recommended), and create a password by following the on-screen prompts.

3.Google Services must be enabled.

After you've logged in, a prompt may appear asking if you would like to allow Google Backup, Location Services, and Sync. Depending on your preferences, you may turn these settings on or off.

4.Logging in using Your Google Profile:

After you've logged in, you'll have access to several Google products, including Gmail, Photos, Drive, and Maps. Another option is to use the Google Play Store to get applications.

5.Linking Accounts:

If you have a Google account, you can sync all of your key data, including contacts, calendar events, images, and more, across all of your devices. Your data is safely stored in your Google account, so you won't lose it even if you change phones.

Account Setup with Samsung

You can't use Samsung Cloud, Samsung Pay, Find My Mobile, or any of the other Samsung-exclusive services without a Samsung Account. This is the way to configure it:

1.**Create an Account with Samsung**:

o Signing into a Samsung Account will be asked of you during the first setup. Select Create Account and then follow the on-screen prompts if you aren't already logged in.

to agree to Samsung's terms and conditions, you must supply an email address, set a password, and complete the registration process.

2.**Login with Existing Account**:

o To log in using your existing Samsung Account, just provide your credentials.

Press the "Forgot Password?" button if you've forgotten your password. back to its factory settings.

3.**Account Perks from Samsung**:

Save all of your important data (pictures, contacts, messages, and more) to the cloud with Samsung Cloud Storage. This way, you can access it even if you misplace your smartphone.

o Find My Mobile: Track down your misplaced or stolen phone and remotely lock or delete all of its data.

o Samsung Pay: Enable Samsung Pay on your phone and use your debit or credit card to make safe purchases.

4.Backup and Sync:

You may transfer all of your data from your old Samsung smartphone to your new phone by logging in with your Samsung Account.

5.The Samsung Account Management Process:

· Go to Settings > Accounts and Backup > Manage Accounts to access and manage your Samsung Account. Update your account information, add an extra layer of protection with two-factor authentication, and see all of your linked devices here.

Getting the Samsung Galaxy A16 connected to Wi-Fi and your accounts is a breeze with these simple steps to follow throughout the setup process.

The User Interface and Navigation

Once you acquire the feel of the touchscreen, navigating your Samsung Galaxy A16 is a breeze. All of your device's operations, including opening applications, navigating displays, and accessing settings, are controlled by touch gestures.

Interface Controls (Swipe, Tap, Pinch, etc.)

With the Samsung Galaxy A16, you may easily interact with the phone using a variety of touchscreen gestures. If you can master these motions, navigating will be a breeze.

1.Tap:

o What it is: A fast tap, or a single touch on the screen.

o When to use it: Launch applications, pick things, or hit buttons (such typing or choosing an icon) with a tap. For instance, you may activate an app by tapping its icon, or begin typing by tapping text areas.

2.Drag and drop:

o Swiping is a way to move your finger horizontally over the screen.

• When to apply it:

To move between various Home Screen pages or open applications, swipe either left or right.

From the bottom of the screen, swipe up to enter the App Drawer, which is where all your apps are stored.

Open the Notification panel or Quick Settings by swiping down from the top of the screen.

3.A pinch:

o Description: To make a pinch motion, bring your index fingers together on the screen.

• When to apply it:

To get a closer look at an object, pinch the screen when using the Camera or Google Maps.

Home Screen: You may see a list of all your Home Screens and rearrange icons by pinching the Home Screen.

4.Increase in size or scope:

The action entails spreading two fingers apart and is the inverse of pinching.

o When browsing photographs, maps, or webpages, use it to zoom in.

5.Refrain from:

What it is: Keeping your finger pressed to a certain area of the screen for an extended period of time.

o When to utilize it: Pressing and holding can offer more choices on icons or applications. To remove or reorganize an app, for instance, you may hold its icon on the Home Screen.

Control Panel Design and Personalization

Every day, you'll be interacting with your widgets and applications from the Home Screen. Your smartphone will function more efficiently once you learn to personalize and arrange your Home Screen.

1.**A General Sketch of the Main Menu**:

You may swipe between different pages or panels that make up your Home Screen.

You should be able to find the Phone, Messages, and Camera apps—among others—on the first page by default.

2.**Page Insertion and Removal**:

o Adding: In order to add a new page to the Home Screen, simply slide to the right on the Home Screen until you see the option to Add Page. To make things more organized, you may add more than one page.

o Deleting: Grab an empty spot on the Home Screen, press and hold the page you wish to remove, and then hit the minus sign.

3.**App Graphics**:

o Drag an app's icon to the spot you want it on the Home Screen by tapping and holding its icon.

Create folders or reorganize applications on various pages. Just drop one app into another to make a folder.

4.Importing Add-Ons:

You may access information or manage certain features without launching the complete program by using widgets, which are miniature, interactive applications. Press and hold an empty space on the Home Screen to bring up the Widgets menu; from there, choose the widget you like.

Widgets like clocks, calendars, weather, and controls for music players are common.

5.Wallpaper Change:

o Select Wallpaper from the Home Screen's menu after pressing and holding an empty spot to personalize your wallpaper. Use one of the pre-installed wallpapers or select a picture from your collection.

Additionally, you have the option to select a new background image for both the Lock Screen and the Home Screen, or even configure a dynamic wallpaper that evolves as the day progresses.

6.**Overarching ideas**:

Themes also allow you to personalize your phone's appearance. You may change the fonts, backgrounds, and icons by browsing the themes in the Settings > Wallpaper and Themes menu.

Status Bar Utilization

On top of your Samsung Galaxy A16, you'll see the Status Bar, which shows important information about your device's current condition. You may stay abreast of your phone's happenings by learning to read the status bar's symbols and indicators.

1.**The Contents of the Status Bar**:

o Time: The upper-right corner shows the current time.

The battery symbol displays the current level of your battery. When your phone is charging, you'll see a lightning bolt in the symbol.

You can see how strong your mobile network connection is by looking at the signal bars.

o Wi-Fi: If you have a wireless network connection, you can see it by looking for the Wi-Fi icon.

o Bluetooth: A sign representing Bluetooth will show up if it is enabled.

o On the other hand, a "circle with a line" indicator shows up when you enable Do Not

Disturb, which means that notifications are muted.

o When applications are making use of your location services, a little location pin icon will be displayed.

o In the status bar, you'll see little symbols representing any new alerts (emails, texts, missed calls, etc.).

2.**How to Get to Quick Settings**:

o Swipe down from the screen's top to access the Quick Settings menu. Access your device's Wi-Fi, Bluetooth, Do Not Disturb, and other settings with ease from this screen.

Touch Edit under the Quick Settings to add or remove choices, and you'll have access to more settings.

3.Region of Notification:

Sliding down from the top of the screen opens the Notification Panel, where you may read detailed notifications.

o Alerts may be set up to receive text messages, emails, app updates, and other types of messages. To access the associated app, simply press the notice; to dismiss it, simply swipe it away.

The App Drawer and Affect Management

You can find every program you've loaded on your device in the program Drawer. You can't have your phone's organization without it. Get to know your apps with these simple steps:

1.Launching the Disk Utility:

Scroll up from the bottom of the Home Screen to access the App Drawer. All of your applications will be shown in a grid layout.

o To locate a particular program, you may either scroll down the list or use the search box on top.

2.Directorsies for Applications:

Apps may be neatly organized by making folders. This is accomplished by tapping and holding an icon for one program, and then dragging it over another app to form a folder. Feel free to give the folder a name (such "Games" or "Social") and then add more applications to it.

Use folders to arrange your programs in a way that's easy to find and use.

3.Deleting Applications:

o Locate the program you wish to delete in the program Drawer, then tap and hold its icon to uninstall it. After a menu displays, choose Uninstall and then confirm your selection.

Go to Settings > applications to remove applications as well.

4.App Reorganization:

Easily reposition an app's icon in the App Drawer or bring it to the front screen by pressing and holding on it.

One option is to organize your programs in folders within the App Drawer, while another is to arrange them in the most accessible spots.

Getting to the Fast Settings

To make quick adjustments to critical settings, you can use the Quick Settings Panel instead of the complete Settings menu. Here's how to utilize it: It's accessible from the top of the screen.

1.**Accessing Basic Preferences**:

o Swipe down from the screen's top to access the Quick Settings Panel. Doing so opens a menu where you may manage several settings, including Wi-Fi, Bluetooth, Do Not Disturb, and more.

2.**Possible Actions**:

o Wi-Fi: Manage your Wi-Fi settings, connect to networks, and turn it on and off.

o Bluetooth: To connect devices, turn Bluetooth on or off or go into Bluetooth settings.

o Turn on or off "Do Not Disturb" to silence all incoming calls and notifications.

For an immediate light source, activate the flashlight.

For a seamless period of inactivity, toggle Airplane Mode on and turn off all wireless connections.

Power Saver: You may lower power usage by enabling or disabling the power saver mode.

To stop the screen from turning, you may use the rotation lock feature. You can choose between a portrait or landscape mode.

3.Improving and Extending Quick Settings:

By default, certain options could be hidden. To access more settings, use the down arrow on the Quick Settings menu.

Tap Edit (often a pencil icon) and move the toggles you use most frequently to the top of the list to modify which settings display in Quick Settings.

4.Gaining Access to All Settings:

o To access the whole Settings menu, touch Settings located at the bottom of the Quick Settings panel if you want more complex configuration options.

Learn the ropes of the Samsung Galaxy A16's touch screen navigation, home screen customization, app management, status bar, and quick settings in this introductory part. Once you've mastered these capabilities, using the gadget will be a breeze!

Calling People and Texting Them

Your Samsung Galaxy A16's capacity to make and receive calls and messages is a fundamental feature. The procedures for carrying them out and optimizing your communication features are detailed below.

Device Management

If you want your Samsung Galaxy A16 to operate smoothly and safely, you need to manage it properly. Here you can find instructions to help you manage your smartphone, from installing apps to configuring security features.

Chapter 2: Application Installation and Removal

Keeping your apps organized is crucial for keeping your phone efficient. Your Galaxy A16 app management guide: installing, updating, and removing apps.

1.**App Installation**:

o The Google Play Store is where most people get their app needs met. Launch the Play Store by navigating to your device's app drawer. Next, look for the software you desire and hit on Install.

The Samsung Galaxy Store is a good place to get Samsung-exclusive applications and themes. Launch the Galaxy Store, type in the app's name, and then hit the Install button.

Apps that don't have official stores can be installed manually by downloading their

APK files, which are known as side-loading apps. Make sure that the option to "Install Unknown Apps" is checked in the following menu: Settings > Apps > [App Name].

2.**Deleting Applications**:

o Push and hold the icon of the app you wish to uninstall in the App Drawer after opening the App Drawer. Among the choices that show up, choose Uninstall.

o Through the Settings menu, navigate to Apps, locate the app you wish to remove, press on it, and then choose Uninstall.

3.**Overseeing App Access Controls**:

Apps may be granted or denied access to many types of data, including your camera, location, and microphone. Navigate to Settings > Apps, pick an app, and then touch

Permissions to make changes to its permissions.

Application (System) Updates

If you care about security, performance, and getting your hands on new features, you must keep your device's software updated. Get the latest version of your Samsung Galaxy A16 here.

1.**Verifying Updates to Software**:

to access the software update, go to Settings.

To see whether your phone has any available updates, tap the Download and Install button.

Downloading and installing an update will be prompted to you if one is available. Before you update, make sure your phone is on a reliable Wi-Fi network and has a good amount of battery life, preferably more than 50%.

2.Updates for the System Installation:

Click Install to start the installation after downloading. To apply the update, your phone will restart.

It normally just takes a few minutes to apply system updates. Your phone will restart with the most recent OS version when the update is finished.

3.Making Software Updates Automatic:

· Go into the Software Update settings and turn on Auto Download over Wi-Fi if you want updates installed automatically. Your phone will automatically download updates whenever it's connected to Wi-Fi, allowing you to install them whenever it's convenient for you.

Data Backup
If your device becomes broken, lost, or reset, you must have a backup of your data. The Galaxy A16 has the following backup options:

1.**Cloud by Samsung**:

Data such as contacts, calendar, images, and app data can be backed up by Samsung through their cloud service. Select Samsung Cloud from the Backup and Accounts menu in Settings.

o Choose which files to back up by tapping the Back Up Data option.

2.Backup with Google:

You can back up your applications, contacts, and settings using Google Drive. Backup My Data is an option under Backup and Restore in the Backup and Accounts section of the Settings menu.

Make sure that Back Up to Google Drive is enabled so that you can back up all of your app data, settings, and more.

3.**Custom Backup**:

Transferring media files to a computer or external storage (such as an SD card or USB drive) allows you greater control when backing up images and movies.

4.**Accessing Third-Party Devices**:

Use an SD card or a USB OTG drive as an external storage option to back up large files or apps. You may manually move files from your phone's internal storage to the storage device by connecting it to your phone.

Phone Reset to Factory Settings

By erasing all user data, applications, and settings, a Factory Reset returns your phone to its factory defaults. If you are looking to sell your gadget, fix problems, or start again, this will be helpful.

1.**Prior to doing a factory reset**:

o Make sure you have saved a copy of all your valuable data, including images, videos, contacts, and more.

o To protect your privacy, sign out of your Google and Samsung accounts.

2.Simple Steps to Reset to Factory Settings:

Reset can be found under Settings > General Management.

o Look over the details that show up after tapping Factory Data Reset.

o When asked, provide your PIN or password by tapping the Reset button.

Your smartphone will reset once you confirm by pressing Delete All.

3.Following the Reset:

· Your device will restart to the setup screen after the reset is finished. If you have backed up your data earlier, you will need to log in with your Google Account and Samsung Account in order to recover it.

Chapter 3: Lock Screen and Security Options

Your data and Galaxy A16 will be safe from prying eyes once you set up the device's security features.

1.**Secure Screen Settings**:

Access the wallpaper, notifications, and security settings for the lock screen by going to Settings > Lock Screen.

o You have the option to turn on or off the Always On Display function, which allows you to see the clock, alerts, and other information even when the screen is turned off.

2.Different Sorts of Screen Locks:

o Swipe: Unlock easily with no security measures required.

To unlock your phone, you need to draw a specific pattern.

o PIN: Use a numerical PIN (4-16 digits).

Choose a robust string of letters and numbers to use as your password.

o Select your desired technique for setting up a lock screen by navigating to Settings > Lock Screen > Screen Lock Type.

Introduction to Passwords, PINs, or Patterns

Your device is more secure when you use a PIN, pattern, or password. This is the way to configure it:

1.Pin Configuration:

o Select Screen Lock Type from the Lock Screen menu in Settings.

choose PIN and input a PIN between 4 and 16 digits long. A confirmation of the PIN will be requested of you.

2.Establishing a Pattern:

o Click on Pattern and then sketch your own pattern onto the grid. To verify it, you'll have to draw the exact same pattern twice.

3.Create a Secure Password:

o Select Password, then input a mix of letters, numbers, and symbols to establish a safe password. Type the same password in again to confirm.

Recognition by Facial Expressions and Fingerprints

By enabling biometric authentication methods like fingerprint and face recognition, you can make your phone even more secure and convenient to use.

1.Fingerprint Recognition System Configuration:

find Fingerprints in the Settings menu, then go to Biometrics and Security.

o Scan your fingerprint by tapping the Add Fingerprint button and then following the on-screen prompts.

Once you've added your fingerprint, you'll be able to use it to unlock your phone and verify additional operations, such as approving payments.

2.Installing Face Recognition Software:

o Go to Settings > Biometrics and Security > Face Recognition.

Press Register Face and then scan your face according to the on-screen prompts.

o After registration, you may unlock your phone using facial recognition.

Track Your Device with Find My Mobile
Find My Mobile is a useful program that allows you to remotely wipe, lock, or trace your stolen or lost Samsung Galaxy A16.

1.Getting Started with Find My Mobile:

Select "Find My Mobile" from the biometrics and security menu in the Settings app.

To enhance tracking and security, log in with your Samsung Account and turn on

Remote Unlock, Remote Controls, and Send Last Location.

2.**Monitoring Your Device**:

Go to any web browser and enter your Samsung account credentials to access the Find My Mobile website (findmymobile.samsung.com) in the event that your handset goes missing.

Tracking, Locking, and Erasing your device are all possible through the internet. Ringing your phone might also assist in finding it.

Follow these steps under Device Management to get your Samsung Galaxy A16 ready for backup, performance, and security. In order to manage your device effectively, it is essential to follow these steps when installing apps, backing up data, or securing your phone.

Superior Functions

A plethora of cutting-edge capabilities enhance the Samsung Galaxy A16's usability, multitasking capabilities, and productivity. Here we'll go over the ins and outs of using these features to make your phone more useful and fun to use.

Dual-Window Mode: Run Two Apps Side by Side

By enabling Multi-Window Mode, you are able to run two applications side by side. Using this function, you may multitask well, for example, viewing a video while reading your email or conversing online.

1.How to Use Multi-Window Mode:

Launch your preferred app.

Select Recent Apps by tapping the square icon located in the screen's bottom left corner.

o In the recent applications view, press the app icon at the top of the app preview, and select Open in Split Screen View.

o Select the second app you wish to open from the list of recent applications or search for it in the app drawer.

You'll now see a split screen, allowing you to use both programs simultaneously.

2.Maximizing or Minimizing the Window:

By sliding the separator between them, you may change the size of each application window. You can adjust its height to make more room for the app you're currently using.

3.Exiting Multi-Window Mode:

If you want to go out of this view, you may either hit the home button to go back to the main menu, or you can drag the divider to the top or bottom of the screen.

Making use of Bixby AI

Developed by Samsung, Bixby is a voice assistant that can be used to access information, complete tasks, and control the phone simply by speaking to it.

1.Bixby Installation:

o To activate Bixby, press and hold the Bixby button (if your device has one) or say "Hi Bixby" to wake it up.

o If you're using the Bixby button, press and hold it to start interacting with Bixby.

You will be asked to log in with your Samsung account and provide the required permissions if Bixby has not been configured yet.

2.Primary Bixby Instructions:

How's the weather looking today, Bixby?"

Hello Bixby, please launch YouTube.

"Hey Bixby, could you please text John?"

Hey Bixby, make sure to set your alarm for 7:00 AM.

o Bixby Vision: Scan objects and photos in real-time with Bixby to obtain translations and comprehensive information.

3.**Bixby Routines**:

o To automate tasks, you can make your own Bixby Routines. Turn off Wi-Fi when you're not at home and put your phone on "do not disturb" when you go to the office.

Settings > Advanced Features > Bixby Routines is where you can configure your behavior.

Desktop Mode for Samsung DeX

With Samsung DeX, you can transform your Samsung Galaxy A16 into a mobile desktop. For those who like to work or watch media on their phones with a bigger screen, keyboard, and mouse, this is a must-have accessory.

1.Setting Up Samsung DeX:

If your smart TV is suitable, you can use Samsung DeX wirelessly. Alternatively, you may use a DeX cable or a DeX station to connect to a monitor.

You can use the adapter that came with your Galaxy A16 to hook it up to a monitor, or you can use Miracast to connect it wirelessly to a TV.

When you connect your phone to the internet, its interface will transform into a desktop-like environment. This will allow you to access windows programs and carry out operations similarly to those on a personal computer.

2.**With DeX**:

o Navigate the screen with the help of the keyboard and mouse. You may drag and drop programs into different windows, access files, and more.

On the other hand, you have Samsung DeX for PC, which lets you turn your phone into a desktop by connecting it to a Windows or macOS computer.

3.Closing the DeX Window:

o To exit DeX Mode, just disconnect the cable, press the home button on the phone, or select Exit DeX on the screen.

Making Use of Linked Apps and Split Screen

You can multitask even easier with features like Split Screen and App Pairs. App Pairs allow you to rapidly open two apps in Split Screen Mode.

1.How to Use Split Screen:

o As noted before in the Multi-Window Mode section, you may drag one program to the top or bottom of the screen to utilize it alongside another app.

o You may run two programs side by side on the same screen by enabling Split Screen mode.

2.Using App Pairs:

You may make your own unique combinations of apps that you use together often by using Samsung's App Pair feature.

o Launch both applications in Split Screen mode. Then, in the Edge panel, which can be accessed by swiping from the screen's edge, tap the App Pair icon, which looks like two overlapping squares. This will create an App Pair.

After you've created the app pair, you can use the App Pair button in the Edge panel to start the two applications simultaneously.

3.Leaving the App Pair or Split Screen Mode:

o To go out of the screen, move the divider to the top or bottom. To go to a specific app, use the recent apps button.

Capturing Screenshots and Recording Screencasts

To record what's going on your screen or take screenshots, the Samsung Galaxy A16 has you covered.

1.Taking Screenshots:

To take a screenshot using the hardware method, press and hold the power button and the volume down button at the same time for a brief period.

o Palm Swipe: Enable the Palm Swipe to Capture feature in Settings > Advanced

Features > Motions and Gestures. To capture a screenshot, just slide your finger across the screen.

o From the Gallery app, you can quickly access the screenshot for viewing, editing, or sharing.

2.Screen Capture:

· To access Quick Settings and begin screen recording, slide down from the top of the screen.

to open the screen recorder, which resembles a camera, tap on it. After you've made your selections for the recording's audio and video quality, hit the Start button.

Tap Stop when you're done, and your recording will be saved in the Gallery app.

Operation by Speech and Verbal Instructions

You can control your Samsung Galaxy A16 with your voice thanks to its advanced voice control features. If you're driving or otherwise occupied with other tasks that need your hands, this feature will come in handy.

1.Invoking Bixby with Your Voice:

Like we said before, Bixby allows you to give voice instructions. Tell them, "Hi Bixby, open Settings" as well as "Hi Bixby, send a message to [contact name]."

2. Google Assistant:

Press and hold the Home button or speak "Hey Google" to activate Google Assistant if you like it. Make use of it to carry out activities, ask inquiries, and establish reminders.

Head over to Settings > Google > Search, Assistant & Voice > Google Assistant to personalize Google Assistant.

3.The Ability to Hear:

The built-in Voice Assistant from Samsung is designed to help people with visual impairments, in case they have trouble utilizing the touch screen. Navigate to Settings > Accessibility > Screen Reader > Voice Assistant to enable spoken feedback for all interactions.

Multitasking, improved accessibility, and greater control through voice and desktop-like experiences are just a few of the ways in which the Samsung Galaxy A16's advanced features may expand your phone's capabilities. These capabilities let you to make the most of your smartphone, whether you're using Split Screen to multitask, recording a lesson, or using Bixby to organize your day.

Senior-Friendly Accessibility Features

For the elderly who may have trouble seeing, hearing, or moving around, Samsung has designed the Galaxy A16 with many accessibility features to meet their needs. These adjustments improve the device's usability and make navigating it easier.

Making Accessibility Settings Active and Personalizable

These are the procedures to complete in order to use all of the accessibility features on your Galaxy A16:

1.**Navigate to the Accessibility Options**:

Accessibility may be found in the Settings menu.

o All the choices meant to make things more accessible for people with various requirements may be found here.

2.**Making Things More Accessible**:

o You may activate a number of features, such as magnification, sound changes, visual upgrades, and more, when you access the Accessibility menu. You may adjust the parameters to suit your needs, and they will be implemented instantly.

Hand Motions for Magnification
Zooming in on the screen with the Magnification Gestures function makes text and images easier to read for individuals with vision impairments.

1.**Maximization**: How to Make It Happen:

o Select Magnification from the Accessibility menu in the Settings.

Magnification Gestures should be enabled.

2.**The Right Way to Use a Magnifier**:

o After you've enabled the function, you may pinch to zoom in simply touching three times on any part of the screen. After you've zoomed in, you may reposition the magnified region by dragging two fingers across the screen.

Pressing the triple-tap button again will zoom out.

3.Exploring the Options for Magnification:

o Navigate to Settings > Accessibility > Magnification to modify the zoom level and configure the behavior of the magnification, among other options.

Strong Contrast with Huge Font Size

With High Contrast and Large Text enabled, your phone's tiny text and distinguishable components will be easier to read.

1.**Making Large Text Visible**:

Proceed to the following menu: Settings > Accessibility > Display.

To make all of the text on the phone bigger, go to the settings and find the "Large Text" option.

To personalize the font size to your liking, you may also utilize the Font Size slider.

2.**Making High Contrast Possible**:

High Contrast Fonts and High Contrast Themes are also accessible from the Display menu.

To make the text show out more clearly against the backdrop, turn on High Contrast Fonts.

To make your phone easier to read, especially for people with limited eyesight, you may enable High Contrast Themes.

3.Improving Readability by Personalizing the Screen:

To have even more control over the how colors look on your computer, use Color Adjustment or Color Inversion (found under Accessibility > Visibility Enhancements).

Screen Reader to Enable TalkBack

Users with visual impairments can rely on the TalkBack function, a screen reader, to read aloud the text on their screen.

1.The Steps to Turn on TalkBack:

o To access TalkBack, go to Settings > Accessibility.

To activate the functionality, simply toggle on TalkBack. To confirm that you wish to activate this service, you might get a prompt.

2.Calling on TalkBack:

o When you turn on TalkBack, your phone will begin to read out loud everything you type or tap on the screen.

As an example, you can hear the name of an app said aloud whenever you press its icon. The screen will read out what you're touching as you swipe or scroll.

o Sliding left or right to switch between things and double-tapping to pick are some of the movements you'll use to navigate TalkBack.

3.Personalizing TalkBack Preferences:

If you want to change the reading speed, pitch, and other choices to make it more comfortable, go to Settings > Accessibility > TalkBack > Settings.

Aids for Hearing and Modifications to Sound Balance

You may change the sound balance and link your hearing aids straight to your Galaxy A16, making it ideal for people with hearing difficulties.

1.Hifi System Connections:

Some Bluetooth hearing aids are compatible with Samsung phones. To connect your hearing aids to your mobile device:

Select Settings, then Accessibility, and finally Hearing.

Connect your hearing aids via Bluetooth by tapping on Hearing aids and following the on-screen directions.

When you're ready to sync your phone and hearing aids, the audio will be sent directly to your ears for enhanced clarity.

2.Changing the Level of Ambience:

To change the sound balance, go to the Accessibility settings, then go to the Hearing area.

If you're experiencing hearing loss in one ear, you can change the left and right audio balance using the slider.

3.One-Tone Sound:

Turning on Mono Audio will merge the two stereo channels into one, which is helpful for people with unilateral hearing loss. If you do this, you can be confident that both of your ears will pick up every sound.

o Tap on Accessibility, then Hearing, and finally Sound Balance in the Settings menu. Turn on Mono Audio.

A User-Friendly Interface for Elderly People

With Samsung's Simple Mode interface, icons are magnified, menus are simplified, and navigation is made more simple, making the device easier to use for seniors.

1.**Launching the Basic Mode**:

o Select Simple Mode from the Accessibility menu in Settings.

To activate Simple Mode, simply toss the switch. This will alter the arrangement of the home screen by enlarging icons and rearranging the placement of apps that are used frequently.

2.Employing the Basic Mode:

By eliminating unnecessary elements and highlighting only the most important features and functions, the interface becomes more user-friendly when Simple Mode is turned on.

There's an option to make text bigger and icons appear more visible.

3.Returning to the Original Mode:

o To disable Simple Mode and revert to the default interface, head back to Settings > Accessibility.

Immediate Notifications and SOS Settings

In the event of an emergency, the Galaxy A16 has safeguards that guarantee elders may obtain assistance swiftly.

1.**Launching Serious Warnings**:

Locate the "Emergency Alerts" option in the "Settings... Safety & Emergency" menu.

Important alerts including weather warnings, local emergency bulletins, and more may be received by toggling on Emergency Alerts.

2.**The SOS Feature Setup**:

With the SOS function, you may quickly and easily call a pre-set contact in case of an emergency.

o To activate SOS:

Accessibility, Safety and Emergency, and Send SOS Messages may be found in the Settings menu.

Before you can set up emergency contacts, you must activate the Send SOS Messages function.

To activate the SOS function, quickly press and hold the Power button three times. Your location will be communicated to the people you've designated as emergency contacts.

3.Quick Shift:

In the event of an emergency, the functionalities that are important can be accessed through the battery-saving Emergency Mode.

o Pressing the Power button and then selecting Emergency Mode from the menu will activate Emergency Mode.

The Samsung Galaxy A16 has been thoughtfully developed with senior accessibility features to ensure a more pleasant and easy user experience. These features make sure you can use your smartphone to its full potential while still meeting your specific needs, whether that's bigger text, more contrast, or voice guiding. Samsung simplifies the process of staying connected, safe, and engaged for seniors by providing emergency alternatives and being compatible with hearing aids.

Organizing Files and Storage

Numerous choices are available on the Samsung Galaxy A16 for handling storage, transferring files, and accessing crucial media and documents. This section will walk you through the steps of clearing space, uploading files to the cloud, or copying data to your PC.

Storage Management and Viewing

If you want your phone to stay working smoothly, you need to manage its storage. Manage your files and programs to see how much space is being utilized and then clear it up.

1.**Checking the Usage of Storage**:

Navigate to the following location: Settings > Battery and Device Care > Storage.

Find out how much storage is available, how much is being utilized, and what kinds of data (apps, media, system files) are using space in this menu.

2.Reducing Storage Needs:

To delete cached files, temporary files, and unneeded data and make more space, you may access this option from the Storage screen by tapping Clean Now.

o To view programs or huge files that are consuming a lot of storage, you may tap on programs or Images. You can then transfer or remove them as necessary.

File Transferring Between Mobile Devices and Computers

It is easy to transfer files from your Galaxy A16 to a computer. This is the way it can be done:

1.Employing a USB Cable:

go ahead and plug in your phone's USB cord to your computer.

o To access the File Transfer option in the USB settings on your phone, scroll down from the top of the screen.

o Launch File Explorer on your personal computer, and your Samsung Galaxy A16 will be listed as a device. Files on your phone and PC may be easily transferred using the drag-and-drop feature.

2.Bluetooth technology:

The first step is to enable Bluetooth on your PC and Galaxy A16.

After you've paired your devices, you can use the Bluetooth File Transfer feature to transmit and receive files.

With the Use of Cloud Storage (GDrive and Samsung Cloud)

You may back up your data to the cloud and then view them from any device. When it comes to saving files, images, and videos, you have two options: Samsung Cloud and Google Drive.

1.**Cloud by Samsung**:

find Samsung Cloud in the Settings menu, then go to Accounts and Backup.

Go ahead and enable cloud backup by logging into your Samsung account. Pictures, programs, and settings are all up for grabs when it comes to backing up.

2.Cloud storage from Google:

o Launch the Google Drive app, or get the app from the Play Store if you don't already have it installed.

Tap the plus sign (+) to add files after signing in with your Google account. To Google Drive, you may upload everything from a single picture to a whole folder.

Any device that is linked to your Google account may access the files that you have stored in Google Drive.

Navigating Files: Viewing Images, Videos, and Documents

All of your device's files may be accessed and managed using the File Explorer, often known as the My Files app.

1.**Accessing My Documents**:

launch the My Files app from the drawer of your app device. Images, videos, audio, documents, and more are just some of the file types that it can sort through.

2.**Data Administration**:

o Open a file or folder by tapping on it. With a long press, you may choose many files and then move, copy, delete, or share them.

o Look for files by name using the search box on top.

3.**Making a Directory**:

To enhance the organization of your documents, photographs, and videos, you have the option to create new folders under My Files.

Methods for Eliminating Adopted Apps (Programs) and Files

Deleting unused data and programs from your phone on a regular basis will keep it working smoothly.

1.**Eliminating Data**:

o To delete a file or folder, open the My Files app, find it, and then long-press on it. Then, hit Delete.

o By choosing the remove option after selecting many files, you can simultaneously remove them.

2.**App Removal**:

Access the Apps section in the Settings menu.

Find the program you wish to remove and then tap on the "Uninstall" button. On the other hand, you may uninstall an app from the App Drawer by pressing and holding its icon.

The Web and Social Networks

Never be alone; always be in the know with the help of the web and your favorite social media applications. With the Galaxy A16, using the web and social media is a breeze.

Google Chrome Web Browser

When you turn on your Galaxy A16, Google Chrome will be your default online browser. To personalize your online surfing experience, follow these steps:

1.**Launching Chrome**:

you may open Chrome by dragging it from the App Drawer or by touching its icon on the Home screen.

2.Exploring the Internet:

o Use Google Search or enter the URL of a website into the address bar to locate the desired content.

o To see all open web sites and to move between them effortlessly, tap on Tabs (the square symbol).

3.Changing Chrome's Settings:

o To access Chrome's settings, tap the menu icon (three dots) located in the top right corner. Here you may modify your homepage, remove recently visited pages, and organize your favorites.

Chatting on Social Media Platforms (Instagram, Facebook, Twitter, etc.)

Keeping in touch with loved ones is a breeze with social media. If you own a Galaxy A16, here's how to access the most widely used social networking apps:

1.**Setting Up Social Media Applications**:

Start by going to the Play Store. Then, look for the app you want to install (for example, Facebook, Instagram, or Twitter).

2.**Application Use for Social Media**:

o Launch the app from the App Drawer when installation is complete.

Start perusing feeds, publishing updates, or talking with friends when you log in (or make an account from scratch).

3.Taking Charge of alerts:

Navigate to Settings > Notifications > App Notifications to manage the notifications that social media applications send you. You may change the app's notification settings by finding it in the list.

Quick Searches using Google Assistant

With the aid of Google Assistant, you can do online searches, get information, and do activities just by speaking to your phone.

1.Turning on Google Assistant:

o To activate Google Assistant, either speak "Hey Google" or press and hold the Home button.

2.When use Google Assistant:

Inquire about the weather by asking inquiries such as, "How is it today?""what is the distance to the closest gas station?""

In addition to managing your smart home gadgets, sending SMS, and setting reminders are all possible with Google Assistant.

3.Making Google Assistant Your Own:

customize the voice, languages, and more of Google Assistant by going to Settings > Google > Assistant.

Customizing Your Samsung Galaxy A16

You may make your Galaxy A16 more unique by applying your own style with the many theme, sound, and other customization choices it provides.

Customizing Background Images and Themes

Here are the methods to change your phone's wallpaper and theme:

1.**Wallpaper Change**:

go to the wallpaper setting.

When you want to change your wallpaper, you can pick one from the Gallery, the Default Wallpapers, or Wallpaper Services.

To set it as your wallpaper, tap on the corresponding button.

2.**Evolving Ideas**:

o To access Samsung's theme shop, go to Settings > Themes.

To update the appearance of your phone, you may install a new theme that includes wallpapers, icons, and color schemes.

Personalizing Audio Files and Ringtones

Make sure you never miss a call or alarm by customizing your ringtone and sound notifications.

1.**Customizing Phone Sounds**:

o Select Sounds and Vibration from the Settings menu.

o Go to your music library or the list and pick a new ringtone by clicking the "Ringtone" button.

2.**Personalizing Alerts**:

You have the option to customize the notification sounds for various apps under the Sounds and Vibration section.

Customizing the Home Screen using Extensions

Widgets allow you to access data or applications quickly without opening the program directly.

1.Importing Add-Ons:

o Choose Widgets by tapping and holding on a blank spot on the Home Screen.

Navigate to the widgets list and drop the one you choose into the Home screen.

2.Customizng Widgets:

To resize a widget, just press and hold it after adding it, and then choose Resize.

Creating a System for File Organization

Put your applications in folders on the Home screen or in the app drawer to make them easier to find and use.

1.Making a File Subfolder:

o To place one app on top of another, tap and hold its icon. It will make a folder.

"Social Media" might be a good name for a folder containing applications such as Facebook and Instagram.

2.Piling on More Programs to the Directory:

You can arrange your applications better by dragging and dropping them into a folder.

Turning on the Dark Theme and Night Mode

By using a darker color scheme, Night Mode and Dark Theme make the screen easier on the eyes.

1.Launching the Shadow Theme

activate Dark Mode by navigating to Settings > Display > Dark Mode.

2.Dark Mode Scheduling:

o In the Settings menu, select Display, and then choose Dark Mode Settings to set automatic on and off timings for Dark Mode.

Follow these steps to maximize the potential of your Samsung Galaxy A16 in terms of storage management, internet connectivity, and personalization. With the Galaxy A16, personalizing your smartphone is a breeze, whether you're organizing applications, configuring social media, or creating ringtones.

Tips and Troubleshooting

Here are some typical problems that users of the Samsung Galaxy A16 could face. In this part, you will find advice on how to improve your equipment and answers to the issues you have encountered.

Typical Problems and Their Solutions

Here are some typical difficulties and how to fix them, ranging from network issues to app issues:

1.**Wireless Network Problems**:

Here's what you can do if your phone keeps dropping the Wi-Fi connection:

To verify if Wi-Fi is turned on, navigate to Settings > Connections > Wi-Fi options.

Make sure you are inside the Wi-Fi router's range.

If you want to fix the connection, you can restart your phone and router.

Reconnect after forgetting the network by navigating to Settings > Connections > Wi-Fi > Tapping on the network > Forget. You should then reconnect.

2.Problem with Bluetooth Connection:

o Resolution: In order to resolve issues with Bluetooth connections:

To toggle Bluetooth on and off, navigate to Settings > Connections > Bluetooth.

Before you attempt to link, ensure that the device is in pairing mode.

You need to restart your phone in addition to the Bluetooth component.

3.Problem with the App:

o Approach: In the event that an app stops responding or freezes:

Swipe the app away from the screen that shows your recent applications to close it.

Press Force Stop in the [program Name] menu under Settings if the issue continues, and then restart the program.

4.Decreased Efficiency:

o Method: To fix a sluggish phone, remove unnecessary data from storage or clear the cache.

To enhance performance, navigate to Settings, then Battery and Device Care, and finally, Optimization Now.

Try emptying the cache of applications by navigating to Settings > applications > [App Name] > Storage > Clear Cache.

When Your Phone Freezes, Here's What to Do

Follow these procedures to fix a frozen or unresponsive Samsung Galaxy A16:

1.**Activate Reboot**:

For about 10 seconds, press and hold both the Power button and the Volume Down button at the same time. You won't lose any data as a result of this forced restart.

2.Look for Updates to Your Software:

o Select Download and Install from the Software Update menu in the Settings. You could find a solution to the freezing problem by installing the most recent software update.

3.Resetting the device to factory defaults:

· A factory reset may be necessary if the phone keeps freezing after trying various remedies (more on this below).

Resolving Problems with App Crashes and Slow Systems

Slowdowns and crashes in apps are annoying. To address these concerns, consider the following:

1.Please update the apps:

to access your applications and games, open the Google Play Store, and then press the hamburger menu (three horizontal lines). Apply any available updates to all applications.

2.Remove Applications:

o If an app keeps crashing, try removing it and then installing it again from the Play Store.

3.Make Room for More:

To find out how much space is being utilized, go to Settings > Battery and Device Care > Storage. Remove or reorganize files to make more room on your phone if it's getting short on storage.

4.Disable App Cache:

o Press the Clear Cache button after going to Settings > Apps > [App Name] > Storage. Problems with programs crashing or running slowly can be resolved in this way.

Revamping Performance with Cache Clearing

Although the temporary data stored in a phone's cache helps apps load faster initially, it can eventually build up and cause your device to run slower.

1.Empty the Cache:

o To delete unnecessary temporary files, go to Settings > Storage > Cached Data, and then touch Clear Cached Data.

2.Bring Out Your Best:

o Select Optimize Now from the Battery and Device Care menu in Settings. This will improve speed by removing temporary files and optimizing settings.

Data Recovery from Erasure

Here is how to retrieve data or files that you have erased inadvertently:

1.Cloud by Samsung:

o To restore data that has been backed up to Samsung Cloud, navigate to Settings > Accounts and Backup > Samsung Cloud > Remove.

2.Backup for Google Drive:

Launch the Google Drive app, then choose the folder or file you wish to recover from your Google Drive backups.

3.Use an application that can retrieve lost data:

You might try downloading an app from a third party, such Dr.Fone or DiskDigger, from the Google Play Store. These tools might be able to assist you recover files that you just erased.

Backing up to the factory settings

If you've tried everything else and your phone still isn't operating properly, resetting it to factory settings may fix the issue.

1.Simple Steps to Reset to Factory Settings:

To reset all factory data, go to Settings > General Management > Reset.

Verify the reset by selecting Reset and then following the directions that appear on the screen. Remember to back up your vital information before you start with a factory reset, since it will delete all data on the device.

2.Following the Clear:

You'll have to start the setup procedure all over again once your device restarts after a factory reset.

Convenient Features and Apps

Many helpful applications and functions are pre-installed on your Samsung Galaxy A16; they may assist you in staying organized, maintaining a healthy lifestyle, and finding assistance.

Tracking Your Fitness and Wellness with Samsung Health

Keeping tabs on your food intake, exercise routine, and overall health is made easier with Samsung Health.

1.**When you use Samsung Health**:

o Go to your device's app drawer and open the Samsung Health app.

Keep tabs on pursuits such as jogging, walking, or cycling. If you own gadgets that are compatible, you can also track your heart rate and how well you sleep.

2.**My Fitness Objectives**:

To establish individual fitness objectives like step count, calorie burn, or activity minute totals, go to Samsung Health and then touch on Goals.

3.Monitoring Your Development:

Find detailed information and your progress toward your fitness objectives on the Home screen, where you can also view your progress.

A Note-Taking and Organizing App for Samsung Devices

If you're looking for a way to keep track of ideas, notes, and information, Samsung Notes is an excellent choice.

1.Note Making:

Start a new note by opening the Samsung Notes app and tapping the Create button.

You have the option to type, handwrite, or sketch your notes. Images and audio recordings can also be included.

2.General Remarks:

Make use of Samsung Notes' folders to arrange your notes according to subjects. Additionally, the search box allows you to look for certain notes.

3.Merging Reminders:

o After logging in with your Samsung account, go to the settings and turn on Sync to make your notes available on all of your devices.

Members of Samsung: Accessing Assistance and Criticism

With Samsung Members, you can get help and share your thoughts with the tech company.

1.Members of Samsung who have access:

o Go to your app drawer and open the Samsung Members app.

o Get advice and news, reach out to customer support, and troubleshoot issues here.

2.Obtaining Assistance:

To troubleshoot your phone, check its camera, sensors, and other components using the Diagnostic Tools available to Samsung Members.

3.Giving Criticisms:

To report issues or offer comments on your device experience, use the comments section in the app.

Streamlining Home Device Connections with Samsung SmartThings

Using Samsung SmartThings, you may manage smart home devices that are compatible with it.

1.Getting SmartThings Started:

Access your Samsung account by opening the SmartThings app.

o After you follow the on-screen directions, you may add smart devices to your system, such as lighting, thermostats, or security cameras.

2.Device Management:

You can manage your connected devices, make adjustments to their settings, and set up automated tasks (like turning lights on

and off at certain times) all from inside the
SmartThings app once you've added them.

Gmail, Calendar, Drive, and Other Google Apps

To keep track of your schedule,
correspondence, and files, Google Apps are a
must-have.

1.Calendar on Google:

To set up reminders, appointments, and
activities, use Google Calendar. Integrating it
with your Google account allows you to
monitor all of your devices simultaneously.

2.Google Mail:

Gmail is an email client that lets you
compose, send, and manage messages. To
begin using Gmail, you must first set up your
Google account.

3.Cloud storage from Google:

Upload media files (pictures, movies, documents, etc.) to Google Drive for online storage and sharing. As long as you have a Google account, you may access them from any device.

The offered troubleshooting steps will allow you to fix the majority of problems and maintain optimal performance on your Samsung Galaxy A16. Staying healthy, staying organized, and getting the most of your smartphone are all made easier with the helpful applications and features.

In summary
Anyone from complete tech newbies to seasoned pros can find everything they need in the Samsung Galaxy A16. Anyone can have a great time using this smartphone thanks to

its user-friendly design, accessibility options, and flexible features. Whether you're new to smartphones or have been using mobile devices for a while, the Galaxy A16 will meet your needs.

Setup, personalization, troubleshooting, and using the phone's built-in applications and advanced capabilities are just a few of the important subjects we've covered in this tutorial. The Galaxy A16 has all the features you need to be organized, connected, and productive, from simple navigation to complex features like Samsung DeX and multi-window mode.

From big text options to voice commands, we've highlighted accessibility features that make the phone more intuitive and easy to use for seniors. With these additions, the

Galaxy A16 is likely to be a trustworthy friend to anybody, regardless of their level of technical knowledge.

To get the most out of your Samsung Galaxy A16, follow these steps. Once you do, you'll be able to do anything from making calls and sending texts to taking pictures and staying connected.

Keep in mind that you'll never be without the resources you need to elevate your experience, thanks to Samsung's ongoing software updates and the helpful community. Your Galaxy A16 can adapt to your needs as you add more apps and features, such as Samsung Health for fitness tracking, Google Apps for calendar management, and Samsung Members for access to support.

Have fun discovering all the features of your Samsung Galaxy A16, and if you need any help, feel free to refer back to this tutorial. Have fun discovering!

Legal Notice

The purpose of this Samsung Galaxy A16 User Guide is to offer users with general information on how to operate the device. Even though we've taken great pains to guarantee that the information is correct and current, some features and settings may differ based on the device's software version, upgrades, or regional variants.

Any problems, losses, or damages that may occur as a result of using the information in this guide are not the responsibility of Samsung Electronics. The user assumes all risk when tinkering with the device's settings or features.

Visit the official Samsung Support page or call Samsung customer care for more thorough and specialized assistance.

Not every conceivable circumstance is addressed in this manual. Please check the official Samsung Galaxy A16 Manual or other official resources from Samsung for specialized troubleshooting or advanced functions that are not included.

Users are cautioned to exercise their own judgment and assume full responsibility while utilizing this information.